# How Heavy? How Much?

### by Jared Adams
### illustrated by Mick Reid

HOUGHTON MIFFLIN     BOSTON

Copyright © by Houghton Mifflin Company. All rights reserved.

No part of this work may be reproduced or transmitted in any form or by any means, electronic or mechanical, including photocopying or recording, or by any information storage or retrieval system without the prior written permission of Houghton Mifflin Company unless such copying is expressly permitted by federal copyright law. Address inquiries to School Permissions, Houghton Mifflin Company, 222 Berkeley Street, Boston, MA 02116.

Printed in China

ISBN 10: 0-618-89977-4
ISBN 13: 978-0-618-89977-7

13 14 15 16 17 0940 20 19 18 17 16

4500590856

cheese (5 oz)
turkey (9 oz)
potato salad (12 oz)
apples (2 lb)
oranges (3 lb)
grapes (1 lb)
ice cream (1 pint)
milk (2 qt)
water (1 gal)

My mom asked my brother Max and me to do some shopping for her at the grocery store.

Her list looked strange. I asked my brother about the numbers and letters in parentheses after each item.

Max answered, "They tell us how many units of measurements to buy. You'll learn about these measurements in third grade."

Read·Think·Write Which of these units are used to measure weight?

Our first stop was the deli counter.

Max asked for 5 ounces of cheese, 9 ounces of turkey, and 12 ounces of potato salad.

As the clerk was weighing the food, Max said:

"The amounts of these things weigh less than a pound, so people measure their weight in ounces (oz)."

**Read·Think·Write** What other things would you measure in ounces?

Our next stop was at the produce department.

"Why don't you weigh the fruit?" suggested Max. "We need 2 pounds of apples, 3 pounds of oranges, and 1 pound of grapes."

"What about ounces?" I asked.

"We use pounds (lb) to measure the weight of heavier things," my brother explained.

"There are 16 ounces in 1 pound, so things that weigh more than 16 ounces are usually measured in pounds."

**Read·Think·Write** How much do the apples weigh?

When we left the produce department, we walked past a display of canned juice.

"How many ounces does this can weigh?" I asked, picking one up.

"Actually," said Max, "for containers of liquids, we talk about capacity, or how much the container holds. The capacity of small containers is usually measured in fluid ounces (fl oz).

"This can holds 8 fluid ounces, or 1 cup (c), of juice."

**Read·Think·Write** Which is more, 3 cups of water or 16 fluid ounces of water?

The last things on our list were 1 pint (pt) of ice cream, 2 quarts (qt) of milk, and 1 gallon (gal) of water. As we put the items into the shopping cart, Max said, "Pints, quarts, and gallons are used to measure the capacity of containers of different sizes. I remember there are 16 fluid ounces in a pint, but I forget how many pints there are in a quart or a gallon."

Read·Think·Write  How many pints are there in a quart? How many pints are there in a gallon?

As we walked home with our bags, I said to Max, "It was fun shopping with you, and thanks for telling me about units of measurement. But right now I can't wait to get home—these groceries weigh a ton!"

## Responding

**Vocabulary**

1. Put these units of measurement in order from largest to smallest: pint, fluid ounce, quart, cup, gallon.
2. Which unit of measurement does not fit: pint, gallon, pound, fluid ounce? Why?
3. Jessica and Tyler went strawberry picking. When they weighed their baskets, Jessica's scale read 2 pounds. Tyler's scale read 32 ounces. Who picked more strawberries?
4. Three friends come to Jason's house. Jason divides a 1 pint container of juice into four glasses. How much does he pour into each glass?

**Activity**

Predict Outcomes Find two things in your classroom that you think weigh about 1 pound. Check their weight by placing them on a balance. How close were you?

## This book is for you!

Whether you're worried, excited, or just thankful for something, God wants to hear from you! Use this book to help you talk to Him.

Scripture quotations are taken from the International Children's Bible®.
Copyright © 1986, 1988, 1999, 2015 by Thomas Nelson. Used by permission. All rights reserved.

# How to get the most out of this book!

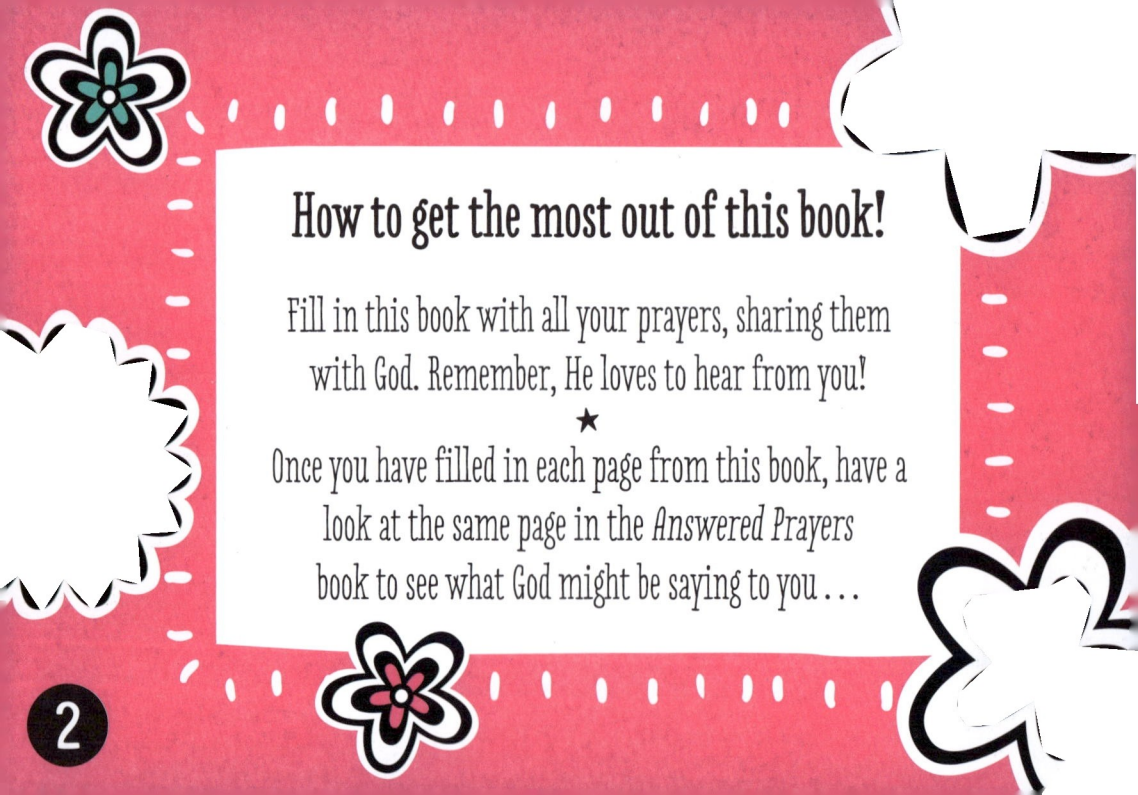

Fill in this book with all your prayers, sharing them with God. Remember, He loves to hear from you!

★

Once you have filled in each page from this book, have a look at the same page in the *Answered Prayers* book to see what God might be saying to you...

SAY HELLO TO GOD! USE THE SPACE BELOW TO WRITE YOUR NAME – THEN DECORATE IT AS MUCH AS YOU WANT!

## WHAT DO YOU LOOK LIKE?

Set a timer for 60 seconds. Start the timer, then draw a portrait of yourself.

## WHAT ARE THE FIVE BIGGEST BLESSINGS IN YOUR LIFE?
### ☑ THE BOXES.

| | | | |
|---|---|---|---|
| family.................................. ☐ | | sports................................. ☐ |
| friends................................. ☐ | | food.................................... ☐ |
| church................................. ☐ | | music.................................. ☐ |
| school.................................. ☐ | | pets..................................... ☐ |
| youth group........................ ☐ | | home................................... ☐ |

# WRITE DOWN THREE THINGS THAT ARE WORRYING YOU AT THE MOMENT AND TELL GOD ABOUT THEM.

1. ......................................................................................

2. ......................................................................................

3. ......................................................................................

# HAVE YOU BEEN KIND TO SOMEONE RECENTLY?

**Write down the three nicest things you have done for others during the past week.**

1. ....................................................................................................

2. ....................................................................................................

3. ....................................................................................................

# ARE THERE THINGS YOU WOULD LIKE TO BE BETTER AT?

**Say this prayer and circle the words that you would most like God's help with.**

Dear God, please can You help me to be more . . .

kind   polite   wise   like You

clever

honest   generous

confident

loving   funny   friendly

**Please help me be the best friend, daughter, classmate, and Christian I can be. Amen.**

# WHAT IS THE FOOD YOU MOST LIKE TO EAT?

**Draw it here, and be grateful for the person who makes it for you.**

# HAVE YOU DONE SOMETHING THAT YOU KNOW MAKES GOD SAD?

**Confess it to God and write it down here.**

# WHO IS YOUR BEST FRIEND?

**Doodle his or her name or draw a picture of your friend here.**

**Think about what your best friend might want God's help with.**

# ALL OF THESE FOODS CAN BE FOUND IN THE BIBLE! DO YOU THINK THEY ARE TASTY OR TERRIBLE?

✓ THE BOXES.

tasty | terrible

- garlic (Numbers 11:5) ............................. ☐ ☐
- mustard (Matthew 13:31) ......................... ☐ ☐
- dates (2 Samuel 6:19) ............................. ☐ ☐
- olives (Isaiah 17:6) ................................. ☐ ☐
- pigeon (Genesis 15:9) ............................. ☐ ☐
- grapes (Nehemiah 13:15) .......................... ☐ ☐

# MY PERSONAL BESTS!

### best school grade
..................................................

### the subject I like best at school
..................................................

### best moment
..................................................
..................................................

### best thing about myself
..................................................
..................................................

## ...TO CHURCH YET?

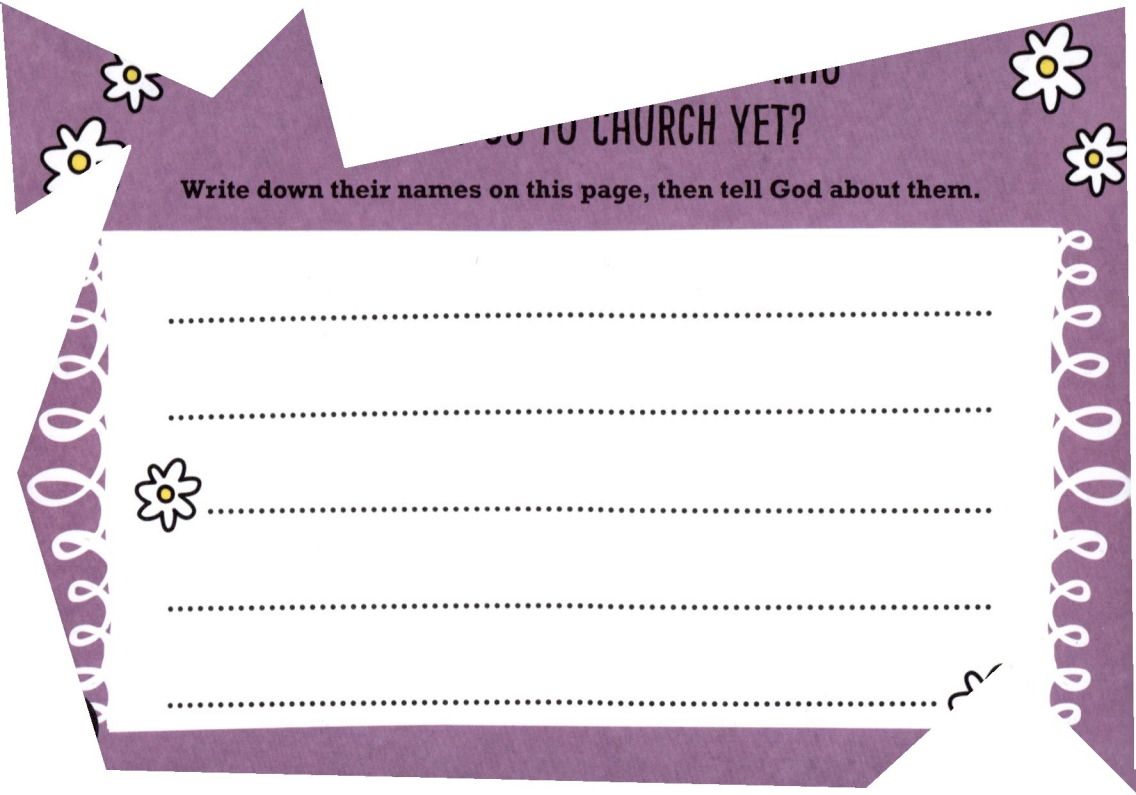

**Write down their names on this page, then tell God about them.**

..................................................................................

..................................................................................

..................................................................................

..................................................................................

..................................................................................

# DO YOU EVER FEEL UPSET? DO YOU GO TO YOUR BEDROOM OR HIDE SOMEWHERE WHEN YOU FEEL SAD?

**Draw a picture of where you like to go when you are feeling sad.**

# WHAT ARE YOU THANKFUL FOR TODAY?
## ✓ THE BOXES.

yummy breakfast ................... ☐

clean clothes ................... ☐

good weather ................... ☐

spent time with friends ................... ☐

fun time at church ................... ☐

watched a great TV show ............ ☐

heard a funny joke ................... ☐

read a good book ................... ☐

# HAVE YOU EVER KEPT A SECRET THAT YOU REALLY WISH YOU COULD TELL SOMEONE? SHARE IT WITH GOD HERE.

**Maybe you could write it in code.**

# ARE YOU AFRAID OF ANYTHING? IF SO, WRITE OR DRAW IT HERE AND TELL GOD ABOUT IT!

# DO YOU KNOW ANY BABIES?

**Maybe you have a baby brother or sister. Thank God for looking after all of the babies in the world. Can you remember . . .**

What time you were born?

..........................................

What day of the week it was?

..........................................

Where you were born?

..........................................

How much you weighed?

..........................................

19

# CAN YOU REMEMBER THE LAST TIME YOU FELT ANGRY?

**What happened and how did you work through your feelings? Scribble some thoughts here.**

DRAW THE OUTFIT YOU LIKE TO WEAR MOST, AND THANK GOD FOR THE CLOTHES THAT YOU HAVE.

# WRITE YOUR NAME AND THEN THINK OF WORDS THAT BEST DESCRIBE YOU, STARTING WITH EACH LETTER OF YOUR NAME.

**(This is sometimes called an acronym.)**

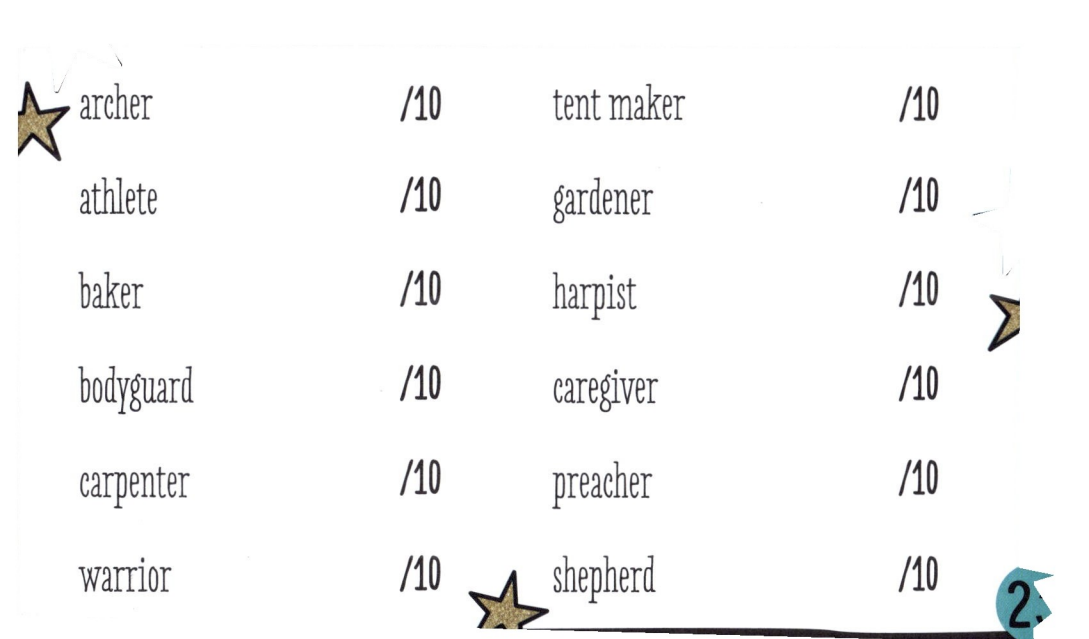

| | | | |
|---|---|---|---|
| archer | /10 | tent maker | /10 |
| athlete | /10 | gardener | /10 |
| baker | /10 | harpist | /10 |
| bodyguard | /10 | caregiver | /10 |
| carpenter | /10 | preacher | /10 |
| warrior | /10 | shepherd | /10 |

# IS THERE ANYONE YOU KNOW WHO NEEDS YOUR PRAYERS?

**List the names of three people who you would like to try to pray for every week.**

1. ........................................................................

2. ........................................................................

3. ........................................................................

# WRITE THE NAME OF A WORSHIP SONG THAT MAKES YOU . . .

**Happy:** ..................................................................

**Think:** ..................................................................

**Sing:** ..................................................................

ARE YOU CONFUSED ABOUT ANYTHING AT THE MOMENT? MAYBE YOU ARE FINDING PART OF THE BIBLE DIFFICULT TO UNDERSTAND. TELL GOD AND WRITE ABOUT IT HERE.

DRAW A PICTURE OF WHAT YOU LIKE TO DO WHEN YOU FEEL TIRED. MAYBE YOU LIKE TO READ A BOOK, WATCH TV, OR TAKE A NAP.

## DO YOU KNOW ANYONE WHO IS FEELING SICK AT THE MOMENT?

**Tell God by filling in the person's name, and then say this prayer.**

Dear God, thank You for loving me and ................. Thank You for medicine, doctors, and nurses. Please can You help make ................. feel better soon and know that You love them and are with them always. Amen.

# THERE ARE LOTS OF WOMEN IN THE BIBLE, AND THEY HAVE MANY DIFFERENT NAMES!

**Circle the names you'd be happiest to have.**

Anna  Deborah  Elizabeth  Rachel  Eve

Hannah  Miriam  Julia  Leah

Lydia  Sarah  Mary  Naomi

Phoebe  Esther  Ruth  Martha

# WHAT ARE THREE BLESSINGS THAT YOU HAVE RECEIVED IN THE LAST WEEK? AS YOU WRITE THEM DOWN, GIVE THANKS TO GOD FOR MAKING THEM HAPPEN!

1. ............................................................................

2. ............................................................................

3. ............................................................................

# CAN YOU REMEMBER A TALK THAT YOU REALLY ENJOYED AT CHURCH?

**Write down what it was about and why you liked it.**

..................................................................

..................................................................

..................................................................

..................................................................

..................................................................

31

# WHAT IS YOUR EARLIEST MEMORY? IS IT HAPPY, SAD, OR JUST WEIRD?

**Doodle or scribble it down here, and tell God how remembering it makes you feel.**

# DID YOU KNOW THAT BY ASKING FOR GOD'S HELP TO LIVE OUR LIVES, WE CAN GAIN THE NINE FRUITS OF THE SPIRIT?

**Look up Galatians 5:22–23 in your Bible, and write down each of these fruits.**

1. ....................................
2. ....................................
3. ....................................
4. ....................................
5. ....................................
6. ....................................
7. ....................................
8. ....................................
9. ....................................

# DEAR GOD, TODAY I FEEL . . .

**Draw a picture of how you feel today.**

# DOODLE THE MOST BEAUTIFUL PLACE YOU CAN THINK OF, AND AS YOU DRAW, TELL GOD WHAT MAKES IT SO SPECIAL TO YOU!

## IF YOU COULD BE ANY OF THESE BIBLE CHARACTERS FOR A DAY, WHO WOULD IT BE?

✓ THE BOXES.

Noah ................................ ☐     Jesus ................................ ☐

Moses ............................... ☐     Peter ................................ ☐

Esther .............................. ☐     King David ......................... ☐

Mary ................................ ☐     John the Baptist .................. ☐

**THE BIBLE SAYS THAT CHILDREN SHOULD RESPECT THEIR PARENTS. DOODLE WHAT YOUR PARENTS DO THAT YOU MOST RESPECT THEM FOR.**

37

# IF YOU COULD BE ANY ANIMAL, WHAT WOULD YOU LIKE TO BE?

**Doodle what you would look like if you were that animal and tell God why you like it!**

# MY PERSONAL WORSTS!

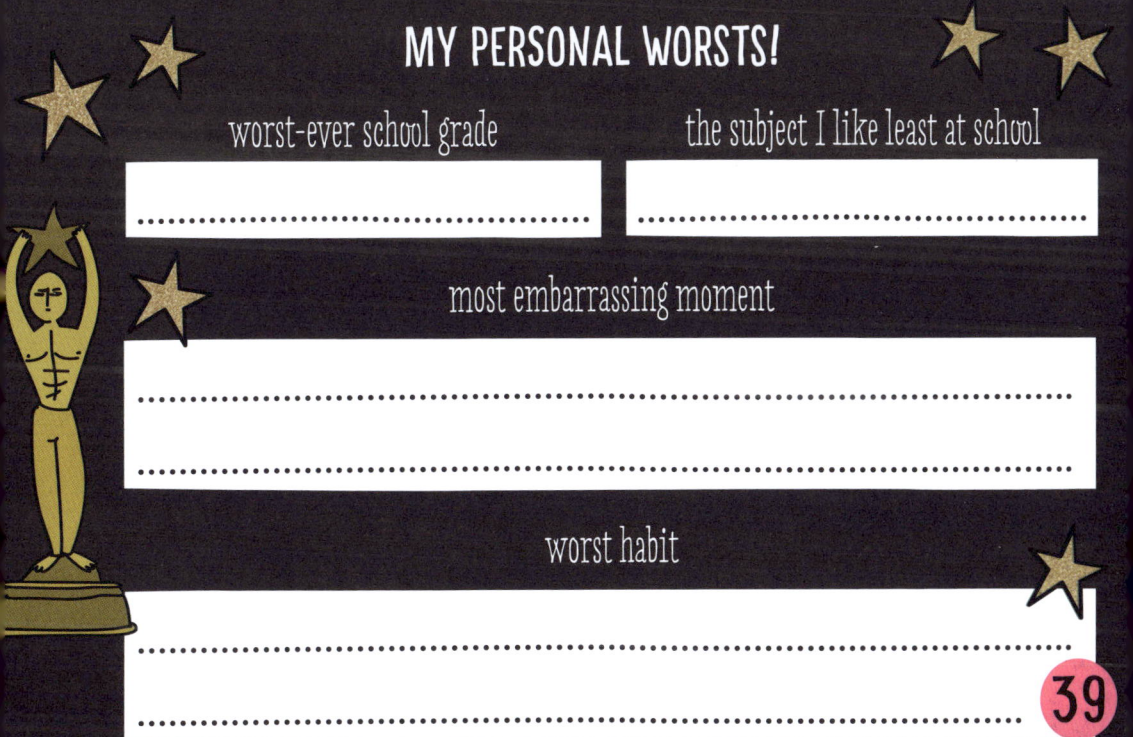

### worst-ever school grade

..................................................

### the subject I like least at school

..................................................

### most embarrassing moment

..................................................
..................................................

### worst habit

..................................................
..................................................

# WHICH SEASON DO YOU LIKE BEST?

..................................................

**List five reasons why, and speak to God about how thankful you are for this season.**

1 ....................................................................

2 ....................................................................

3 ....................................................................

4 ....................................................................

5 ....................................................................

40

# IS THERE A WORD OR PHRASE THAT YOU USE A LOT?

**Write your word or phrase here and doodle around it.**

41

# WHO IS YOUR BEST TEACHER AT SCHOOL?

**Draw a picture of him or her and tell God what makes your teacher so great!**

# WHAT IS THE BEST THING YOUR GRANDPARENT OR AN ELDERLY PERSON HAS TAUGHT YOU?

**Think about what you have learned and thank God for the knowledge.**

........................................................................

........................................................................

........................................................................

........................................................................

........................................................................

# THINK OF ALL THE BIRTHDAY GIFTS YOU HAVE EVER BEEN GIVEN. DID YOU SAY THANK YOU FOR THEM?

What was the most unusual?

..............................................................................

What was the most unexpected?

..............................................................................

Is there one you would keep forever?

..............................................................................

## CIRCLE THE THREE COUNTRIES YOU'D MOST LIKE TO VISIT.

France
China
Italy
Russia
Japan
Australia
Kenya
Brazil
Mexico
Thailand
Spain
New Zealand
Egypt
Greece
India
Iceland
Ireland
Germany
South Africa

45

# WHEN DO YOU LIKE TO PRAY?
## ☑ THE BOXES.

|  | never | sometimes | often |
|---|---|---|---|
| when I wake up | ☐ | ☐ | ☐ |
| with my family | ☐ | ☐ | ☐ |
| when I am happy | ☐ | ☐ | ☐ |
| on my way to school | ☐ | ☐ | ☐ |

|  | never | sometimes | often |
|---|---|---|---|
| at church | ☐ | ☐ | ☐ |
| when I need help | ☐ | ☐ | ☐ |
| before I go to sleep | ☐ | ☐ | ☐ |
| with my friends | ☐ | ☐ | ☐ |
| at Christmas | ☐ | ☐ | ☐ |
| when I am worried | ☐ | ☐ | ☐ |
| before eating dinner | ☐ | ☐ | ☐ |

# CAN YOU NAME THREE THINGS THAT ARE WORTH WAITING FOR?

**If you are struggling to wait, ask God to help you be more patient.**

1. ...........................................................................................

2. ...........................................................................................

3. ...........................................................................................

# DOODLE A PICTURE OF YOUR FUNNIEST MOMENT!

**What happened, who was there, and do you still laugh about it?**

LOL!

LOL!

DO YOU HAVE A BROTHER OR SISTER? OR PERHAPS YOU KNOW PEOPLE WHO ARE SO CLOSE TO YOU THAT THEY FEEL LIKE BROTHERS OR SISTERS? DOODLE THEIR NAMES HERE, AND TELL GOD WHAT YOU MOST LIKE DOING WITH THEM.

# GOD CREATED EVERY PLANT AND FLOWER. HE MADE SOME FOR US TO EAT AND OTHERS FOR US TO ENJOY!

**Circle the flowers that you think are best and thank God for them!**

Daffodil   Iris   Jasmine   Crocus   Bluebell

Violet   Pansy   Tulip   Sunflower

Rose   Daisy   Foxglove   Lavender

Lily

Carnation   Poppy   Honeysuckle   Primrose

# WHAT IS THE MOST BEAUTIFUL THING YOU HAVE EVER SEEN? WHAT MADE IT SO SPECTACULAR? DRAW A PICTURE OF IT HERE.

# DO YOU KNOW THE NAME OF THE LEADER OF YOUR COUNTRY?

**Write it down here and think about three things people need to do to be good leaders.**

........................................

1 ...........................................................................................

2 ...........................................................................................

3 ...........................................................................................

**Thank God for the people who lead us, and pray that they lead in the best way possible.**

# IS THERE SOMEONE YOU HAVE UPSET RECENTLY, SOMEONE YOU NEED TO SAY SORRY TO?

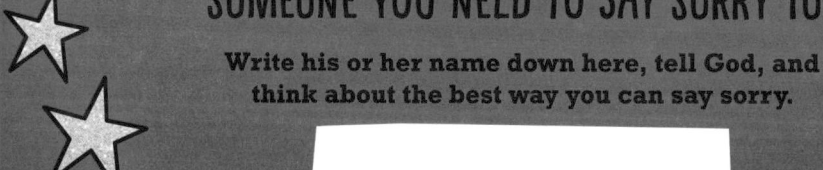

**Write his or her name down here, tell God, and think about the best way you can say sorry.**

# RATE THE THINGS THAT KEEP YOU SAFE EVERY DAY!

**0% means it doesn't keep you safe at all.**
**100% means you are totally safe!**

| | | | |
|---|---|---|---|
| seat belts | ........% | firefighters | ........% |
| police | ........% | warning signs | ........% |
| apples | ........% | winter coat | ........% |
| youth leader | ........% | lifeguards | ........% |
| parents | ........% | smoke alarms | ........% |
| teddy bear | ........% | God | ........% |

# DO YOU KNOW SOMEONE WHO NEEDS TO FEEL GOD'S LOVE AT THE MOMENT?

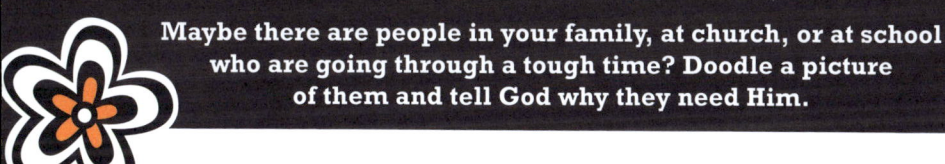

Maybe there are people in your family, at church, or at school who are going through a tough time? Doodle a picture of them and tell God why they need Him.

# GOD IS INCREDIBLE!

**Circle your top five words that describe God and thank Him for being who He is!**

steady  wise  honest  strong

loving  powerful  faithful

caring

amazing  awesome  kind

good  Creator

# IS THERE SOMETHING YOU REALLY DON'T LIKE DOING? MAYBE IT'S CLEANING YOUR ROOM OR FEEDING THE DOG?

**Doodle it here, and think about why you don't like doing it.**

# CIRCLE THE THREE CHARACTERISTICS THAT BEST DESCRIBE YOUR BFF.

funny  generous  confident  caring
curious  excitable
loud  strong
friendly  glamorous  cheerful
moody  happy  grumpy
frosty
adventurous  creative  shy
lazy
dramatic  calm  quiet  silly

# CAN YOU REMEMBER THE LAST TIME YOU WERE SPEECHLESS OR DIDN'T KNOW WHAT TO SAY?

**Doodle what happened here, and think about how it made you feel.**

# WHERE DO YOU GO WHEN YOU NEED SOMEWHERE QUIET TO PRAY?

**Maybe you hide in your bedroom, sit under a special tree in the garden, or go somewhere top secret? Doodle the prayer space you like the most here and think about what makes it a great place to pray.**

## DO YOU LIKE SPORTS AND ACTIVITIES?
## ... THE BOXES.

|  | love | like | don't like |  | love | like | don't like |
|---|---|---|---|---|---|---|---|
| swimming | ☐ | ☐ | ☐ | hockey | ☐ | ☐ | ☐ |
| horseback riding | ☐ | ☐ | ☐ | gymnastics | ☐ | ☐ | ☐ |
| skipping | ☐ | ☐ | ☐ | football | ☐ | ☐ | ☐ |
| running | ☐ | ☐ | ☐ | dancing | ☐ | ☐ | ☐ |
|  |  |  |  | walking | ☐ | ☐ | ☐ |
|  |  |  |  | martial arts | ☐ | ☐ | ☐ |

# HAVE YOU EVER TOLD SOMEONE WHO DOESN'T BELIEVE IN GOD THAT YOU DO?

**Write down his or her name and talk to God about what happened.**

# GOD GAVE US THE TEN COMMANDMENTS TO HELP US LIVE OUR LIVES THE BEST WAY WE CAN.

**Rate how hard it is to keep each of them.
0% means almost impossible. 100% means really easy!**

| | | | |
|---|---|---|---|
| put God first | ……… % | do not hurt other people | ……… % |
| worship only God | ……… % | be faithful | ……… % |
| use God's name with respect | ……… % | do not steal | ……… % |
| remember God's Sabbath | ……… % | do not lie | ……… % |
| respect your parents | ……… % | do not be envious of others | ……… % |

# HOW DO YOU FEEL WHEN YOU HAVE TO DO SOMETHING NEW? IS THERE SOMETHING THAT YOU HAVE NEVER DONE BEFORE THAT YOU ARE AFRAID OF DOING?

**Write it down, and tell God the reasons why you think it might be scary.**

..................................................................................

..................................................................................

..................................................................................

..................................................................................

..................................................................................

# HAVE YOU EVER BEEN LOST OR FELT THAT YOU DIDN'T KNOW WHERE YOU WERE? DID YOU PRAY FOR GOD'S HELP? WRITE DOWN WHAT HAPPENED AND HOW IT MADE YOU FEEL.

..................................................................................

..................................................................................

..................................................................................

..................................................................................

..................................................................................

# IS THERE SOMEONE YOU DO NOT GET ALONG WITH VERY WELL AT THE MOMENT?

**Write his or her name here and tell God why you think you don't get along.**

..............................................

..............................................................................................

..............................................................................................

..............................................................................................

..............................................................................................

# HAVE YOU EVER WON A COMPETITION? MAYBE YOU HAVE ONE COMING UP SOON THAT YOU ARE FEELING NERVOUS ABOUT.

**Tell God about it and ask for His strength and help.**

# WRITE ABOUT A TIME WHEN YOU HAVE PRAYED FOR SOMETHING REALLY IMPORTANT. HOW DID GOD HELP YOU?

..............................................................................

..............................................................................

..............................................................................

..............................................................................

..............................................................................

# WHAT IS YOUR DREAM JOB?
## ☑ THE BOXES.

| | | | |
|---|---|---|---|
| teacher | ☐ | nurse | ☐ |
| pop singer | ☐ | athlete | ☐ |
| journalist | ☐ | veterinary surgeon | ☐ |
| politician | ☐ | fashion stylist | ☐ |
| doctor | ☐ | chef | ☐ |
| hairdresser | ☐ | dance teacher | ☐ |
| full-time mother | ☐ | writer | ☐ |

## WHO IN YOUR FAMILY ARE YOU MOST LIKE?

..................................................................................................................

## IN WHAT WAYS?

..................................................................................................................

..................................................................................................................

..................................................................................................................

..................................................................................................................

# WHAT ARE YOUR HOPES FOR THE FUTURE? HOW LIKELY DO YOU THINK IT IS THAT YOU WILL DO THE FOLLOWING THINGS?

**0% means no chance, 100% means it's going to happen, and 110% means that it already has!**

| | | | |
|---|---|---|---|
| fly into space | ........% | ride a camel | ........% |
| star in a reality TV show | ........% | dye your hair pink | ........% |
| ski in Switzerland | ........% | design a house | ........% |
| swim with a dolphin | ........% | perform in a play | ........% |
| climb a mountain | ........% | meet a celebrity | ........% |

71

# DOODLE A PICTURE OF WHAT YOU ARE MOST THANKFUL FOR IN THE WHOLE WORLD!

72

# ANSWERED PRAYERS

## This book is also for you!

God hears all of your prayers and will always share His answers with you. Sometimes He will say yes, sometimes He will say no, and sometimes He will ask you to wait a while and have faith in Him.

Scripture quotations are taken from the International Children's Bible®. Copyright © 1986, 1988, 1999, 2015 by Thomas Nelson. Used by permission. All rights reserved.

# How to get the most out of this book!

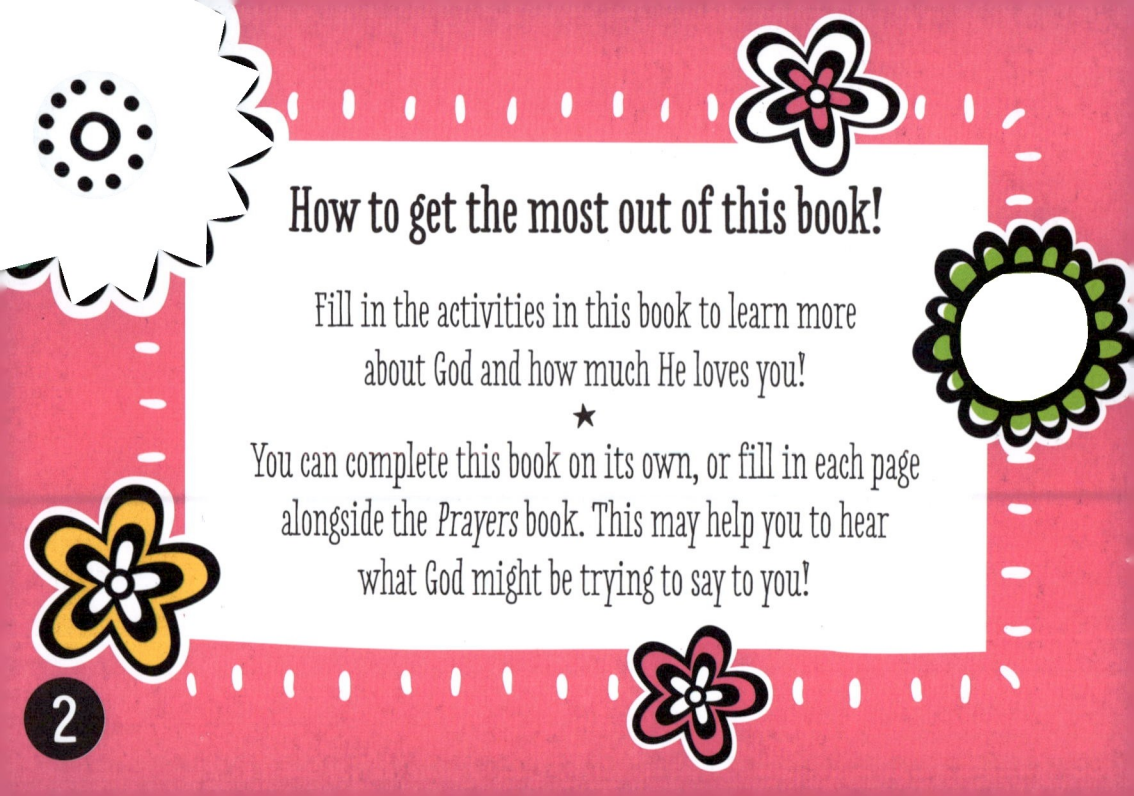

Fill in the activities in this book to learn more about God and how much He loves you!

★

You can complete this book on its own, or fill in each page alongside the *Prayers* book. This may help you to hear what God might be trying to say to you!

# GOD KNOWS YOU BY NAME, AND WHEN HE SPEAKS TO YOU, HE WILL USE IT!

**Look up the verse Isaiah 43:1 and write the rest of it here.**

"Don't be afraid . . .

..............................................................................

..............................................................................

"

..............................................................................

# THE WONDERFUL THING ABOUT GOD IS THAT HE LOVES YOU, JUST THE WAY YOU ARE!

**Circle the words God says about you in this Bible verse and try to remember them.**

The Bible says: "I praise you [God] because you made me in an amazing and wonderful way. What you have done is wonderful. I know this very well" **(Psalm 139:14).**

# WHO DO YOU THINK GIVES YOU YOUR BLESSINGS?

..........................................

**Read James 1:17 and write down why you are thankful for your top five blessings.**

1 ..............................................................................

2 ..............................................................................

3 ..............................................................................

4 ..............................................................................

5 ..............................................................................

# THE BIBLE IS GOD'S WORD FOR US, AND IT HAS LOTS OF TIPS ON HOW WE CAN STOP WORRYING.

**Look up Philippians 4:6 in your Bible, then fill in the missing words.**

"Do not worry about ................. . But pray and ask ................. for everything you need. And when you pray, always give ................. ." **(Philippians 4:6).**

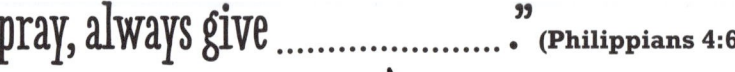

# READ 2 THESSALONIANS 2:16-17. GOD IS VERY PLEASED WHEN YOU DO KIND THINGS FOR OTHERS, AND HE GIVES YOU HOPE, COMFORT, AND STRENGTH WHEN YOU DO!

**What activities would you do if you were really strong?**

..................................................................................

..................................................................................

..................................................................................

..................................................................................

..................................................................................

7

# THANK YOU GOD, FOR MAKING ME...

**Write down the words that best describe you.**

........................................................................................................

........................................................................................................

........................................................................................................

........................................................................................................

## HELP ME TO REMEMBER THAT YOU MADE ME UNIQUE, DIFFERENT FROM ANYONE ELSE, AND THAT YOU LOVE ME JUST AS I AM. AMEN.

THANK YOU, GOD, FOR THE FOOD I LIKE MOST AND FOR ...................., WHO MAKES IT FOR ME. PLEASE HELP ME BE GRATEFUL, EVEN FOR THE FOODS I DON'T ENJOY, LIKE ...................., AND TO REMEMBER TO ALWAYS THANK YOU FOR THE FOOD YOU PROVIDE FOR ME. AMEN.

# GOD HAS FORGIVEN YOU FOR EVERY BAD THING YOU HAVE EVER DONE! HOW DOES THAT MAKE YOU FEEL?

☑ **THE BOXES.**

- happy ☐
- blessed ☐
- excited ☐
- thankful ☐

The Bible tells us that "if we confess our sins, [God] will forgive our sins. We can trust God. He does what is right. He will make us clean from all the wrongs we have done." **(1 John 1:9)**

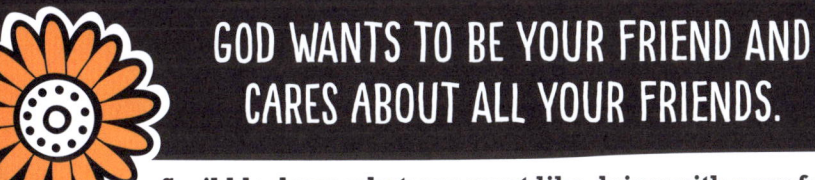

# GOD WANTS TO BE YOUR FRIEND AND CARES ABOUT ALL YOUR FRIENDS.

**Scribble down what you most like doing with your friend and thank God for the fun you have together.**

The Bible says, "Two people are better than one. They get more done by working together" **(Ecclesiastes 4:9).**

# THERE IS A LOT OF FOOD TO BE FOUND IN THE BIBLE!

Look up the following Bible verses and write down the food that you find. As you write, thank God for the food you like!

.................................................... **Numbers 11:5**

.................................................... **Mark 1:6**

.................................................... **Numbers 6:3**

# DEAR GOD, THANK YOU FOR BLESSING ME SO I CAN ACHIEVE MY PERSONAL BESTS...

best school grade

..........................................

the subject I like best at school

..........................................

best moment

..........................................

best thing about myself

..........................................

## ...PLEASE HELP ME TO CONTINUE TO ACHIEVE MY VERY BEST IN EVERYTHING I DO! AMEN.

## GOD WANTS ALL OF YOUR FRIENDS TO TRUST HIM.

**Say this prayer, filling in the names of your friends who do not know Him yet.**

Dear God, thank You for loving me and all my friends. Please help ................... and ................... know more about You and love You too. Amen.

# GOD IS ALWAYS WITH YOU, AND HE LOVES YOU.

**Look up Isaiah 41:10 in your Bible and copy it here.**

# GOD LOVES YOU, AND HE GIVES YOU LOTS OF THINGS IN YOUR LIFE TO BE THANKFUL FOR. HOW CAN YOU BEST THANK HIM?

✓ THE BOXES.

| | | | |
|---|---|---|---|
| praying | ☐ | being kind | ☐ |
| singing | ☐ | smiling | ☐ |
| being happy | ☐ | helping others | ☐ |

# YOU CAN TELL GOD ABOUT ABSOLUTELY EVERYTHING. HE ALREADY KNOWS EVERY SECRET IN THE WHOLE WORLD!

**Look up Psalm 147:5 in your Bible and copy the verse here.**

17

# GOD CONQUERS ALL, SO DO NOT WORRY! DRAW A PICTURE OF GOD DEFEATING WHATEVER YOU ARE AFRAID OF.

# DID YOU KNOW THAT GOD KNEW YOU BEFORE YOU WERE EVEN A BABY?

**Look up Jeremiah 1:5 in your Bible, and then write the verse here to try to remember it!**

"Before I made you...

..................................................................................

..................................................................................

.................................................................................."

## WRITE DOWN THE THINGS THAT CALM YOU DOWN WHEN YOU ARE FEELING ANGRY.

**Remember, God doesn't want us to be angry and will often give us things in our lives to make us feel better.**

..................................................................

..................................................................

..................................................................

The Bible tells us, "Always be willing to listen and slow to speak. Do not become angry easily. Anger will not help you live a good life as God wants."
**(James 1:19–20)**

**READ EPHESIANS 6:14-18 IN YOUR BIBLE, AND DRAW YOURSELF WEARING THE SPECIAL CLOTHING GOD HAS GIVEN YOU.**

**Thank God for these amazing qualities.**

21

THINK OF WORDS BEGINNING WITH G, O, AND D THAT BEST DESCRIBE GOD AND WRITE THEM HERE!

# DO YOU KNOW WHAT YOU WANT TO BE WHEN YOU GROW UP? TALK TO GOD ABOUT WHAT JOBS YOU WOULD BE BEST AT.

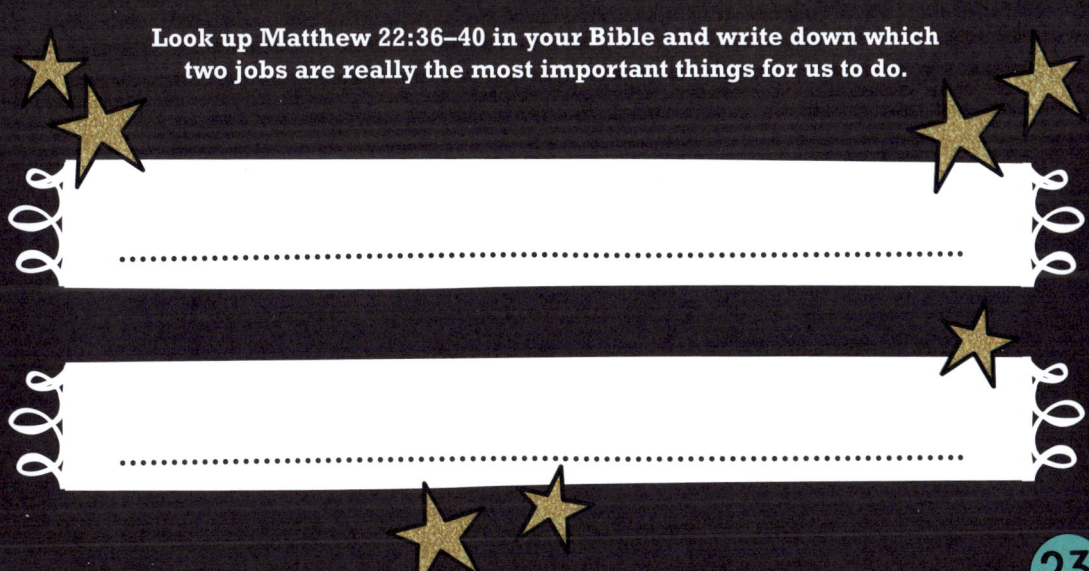

**Look up Matthew 22:36–40 in your Bible and write down which two jobs are really the most important things for us to do.**

..................................................................................................

..................................................................................................

23

# IT IS GREAT TO PRAY FOR OTHER PEOPLE, AND GOD ALWAYS LISTENS!

**Doodle some pictures of what you would like God to do for the people you are praying for.**

# TRY MAKING UP YOUR OWN CHORUS OF A SONG, THANKING GOD FOR MUSIC AND FOR THE SONGS YOU LOVE.

# WHO CAN YOU TALK TO ABOUT WHATEVER IS CONFUSING YOU AT THE MOMENT? SOMETIMES GOD WANTS US TO SPEAK TO THE PEOPLE WHO LOVE US, AND HE GIVES THEM WISE WORDS TO SAY.

**Write the names of three people you can talk to and be honest with. This may be a parent, youth worker, or teacher.**

1. ....................................................................................

2. ....................................................................................

3. ....................................................................................

IN THE BIBLE, MATTHEW 11:28-29 TELLS US THAT GOD HELPS US WHEN WE ARE TIRED AND WANTS US TO REST WHEN WE NEED TO. DO YOU TALK TO GOD BEFORE YOU GO TO SLEEP? DRAW A PICTURE OF THE COMFIEST BED IN THE WORLD!

WE CAN FEEL REALLY SAD WHEN SOMEONE WE KNOW IS SICK, BUT REMEMBER THAT GOD IS ALWAYS WITH US, WHETHER WE ARE HAPPY OR SAD, HEALTHY OR SICK. HE WILL NEVER LEAVE US, AND HE LOVES US VERY MUCH.

Look up Jeremiah 17:14 in your Bible and fill in the missing words.

"Lord, .................. me, and I will truly be healed. Save me, and I will truly be .................. . Lord, you are the one I .................. ." (Jeremiah 17:14)

# THE BIBLE USES MANY NAMES FOR GOD.

**Circle the ones that mean the most to you.**

God	Father	King	Lord

Messiah	Shepherd	Jesus

Creator	Christ	Almighty

Holy One	Light	..................

**What do you think is the best name for God? (You can even add a name not listed above.)**

## CAN YOU THINK OF WAYS THAT YOU CAN BE A BLESSING TO OTHERS THIS WEEK?

..................................................................

..................................................................

..................................................................

..................................................................

..................................................................

# IS THERE ANYTHING YOU WOULD LIKE TO HEAR MORE ABOUT AT CHURCH?

**Write the topic down here and ask God to help you learn more about it.**

..................................................................

..................................................................

..................................................................

..................................................................

..................................................................

**Maybe you could mention the subject to your youth leader.**

# GOD BLESSES US WITH PEOPLE WHO LOVE US OUR ENTIRE LIVES.

**Write down their names here and tell God why you are thankful for them.**

..................................................................................

..................................................................................

..................................................................................

..................................................................................

In Philippians 1:3-4, the apostle Paul writes, "I thank God every time I remember you. And I always pray for all of you with joy."

# WRITE DOWN THE NINE FRUITS OF THE SPIRIT (FROM GALATIANS 5:22-23), AND RATE WHICH ONES YOU MOST NEED GOD'S HELP WITH.

**0% means you think you're doing well with this one.**
**100% means you have never done this before and need God's help!**

| | | | |
|---|---|---|---|
| ............................. | ........% | ............................. | ........% |
| ............................. | ........% | ............................. | ........% |
| ............................. | ........% | ............................. | ........% |
| ............................. | ........% | ............................. | ........% |
| ............................. | ........% | | |

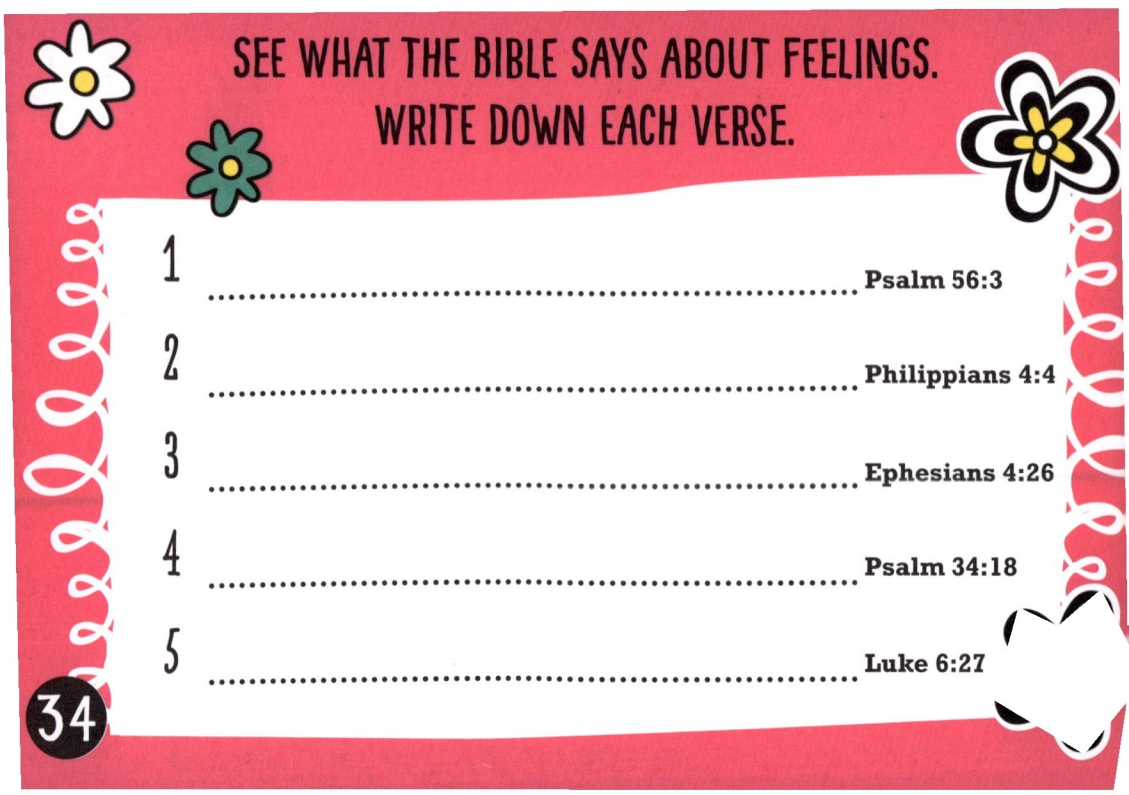

## SEE WHAT THE BIBLE SAYS ABOUT FEELINGS. WRITE DOWN EACH VERSE.

1. .................................................................... **Psalm 56:3**

2. .................................................................... **Philippians 4:4**

3. .................................................................... **Ephesians 4:26**

4. .................................................................... **Psalm 34:18**

5. .................................................................... **Luke 6:27**

# IN YOUR BIBLE, READ REVELATION 22:1-5 AND DRAW A PICTURE OF WHAT YOU THINK HEAVEN WILL LOOK LIKE.

DEAR GOD, THANK YOU FOR ALL THE PEOPLE IN THE BIBLE AND THEIR STORIES. PLEASE HELP ME TO BE MORE LIKE THE CHARACTER I LIKE BEST ( .................... ) BECAUSE

..................................................................................................
..................................................................................................
.................................................................................................. .

AMEN.

# IN THE BIBLE, JESUS SAYS THAT GOD IS OUR FATHER ALMOST 200 TIMES! GOD IS THE PERFECT FATHER. HE WILL ALWAYS LOVE YOU AND YOUR PARENTS AND WILL NEVER LET YOU DOWN!

**Look up 1 John 3:1, write it down, and try to remember it.**

# AS WELL AS CREATING YOU, YOUR FRIENDS, AND YOUR FAMILY, GOD ALSO CREATED EVERY ANIMAL IN THE WORLD!

**Look up Job 35:11 in your Bible to see what God does for His most special creation (you!) and write the answer down here.**

..............................................................................

..............................................................................

..............................................................................

..............................................................................

..............................................................................

# DEAR GOD, HELP ME TO SEE THE GOOD IN THE THINGS I STRUGGLE WITH...

I can learn

..........................................

I have help from

..........................................

I am getting better at

..........................................

Something I don't worry about anymore is

..........................................

## ...AND REMIND ME TO FOCUS ON MY BEST! AMEN.

# GOD IS SO POWERFUL THAT HE CREATED ALL FOUR OF THE SEASONS!

Look up Daniel 2:21 in your Bible and list three other things God can do.

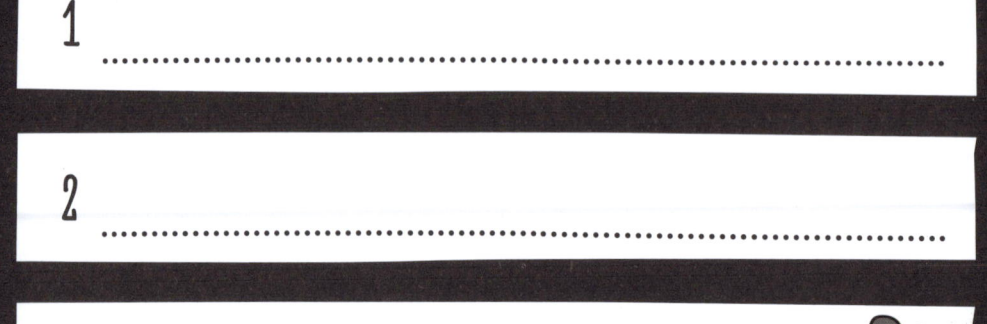

1 ......................................................................................

2 ......................................................................................

3 ......................................................................................

40

DID YOU KNOW THAT THE WORD *LOVE* IS USED MORE THAN 300 TIMES IN THE BIBLE? CAN YOU THINK OF THREE REASONS WHY LOVE IS SO IMPORTANT?

1 ....................................................................................

2 ....................................................................................

3 ....................................................................................

41

GOD LOVES US SO MUCH THAT HE SENT HIS SON, JESUS, TO EARTH TO HELP TEACH US HOW TO LIVE OUR LIVES. CAN YOU THINK OF THREE THINGS THAT GOD HAS TAUGHT YOU?

1. ..................................................................................

2. ..................................................................................

3. ..................................................................................

## PROVERBS 17:6 SAYS THAT GRANDCHILDREN ARE THEIR GRANDPARENTS' REWARD. DO YOU FEEL LIKE YOU ARE A REWARD TO YOUR GRANDPARENTS?

**Doodle what you could do to bring more happiness to their lives.**

# GOD HAS GIVEN US SOME WONDERFUL GIFTS TO HELP US LIVE OUR LIVES!

**From the list below, rank which gifts you would most like to have (1–4). Pray that God gives them to you and helps you make the best use of them.**

| | |
|---|---|
| wisdom | |
| knowledge | |
| faith | |
| healing | |

# GOD LOVES EVERYONE IN EVERY COUNTRY! WHETHER PEOPLE LIVE IN A REALLY BIG CITY OR ON A REMOTE DESERT ISLAND, NO ONE IS TOO FAR AWAY FOR GOD TO REACH.

Write your own prayer thanking Him for the places you have visited and want to visit, and also pray for the people who are experiencing hard times in their own countries.

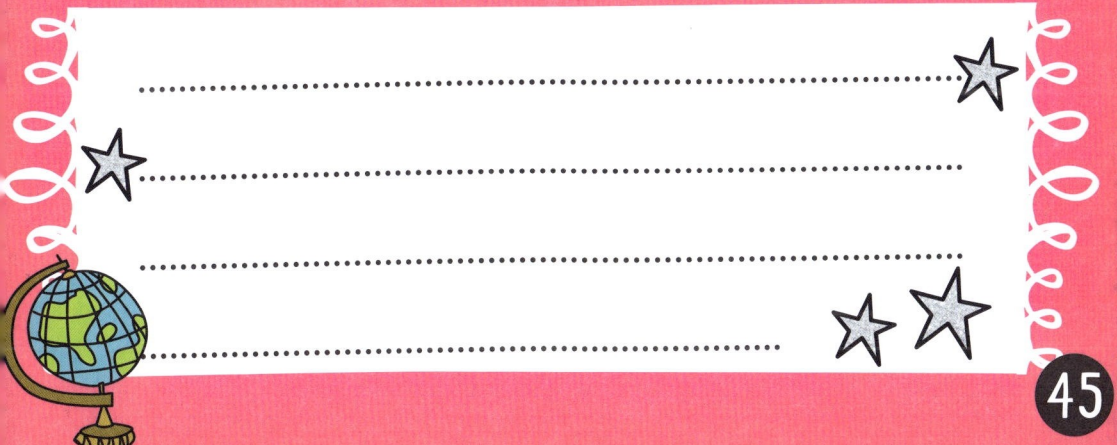

## WOULD YOU LIKE TO PRAY MORE?

**God wants to speak to you as much as possible! Why don't you pray this prayer, filling in where you would like to pray more, and then ask God for His help.**

Dear God, thank You for wanting to speak to me all day and for being involved in my life. I love how much You love me. Please help me to speak to You whenever I can. I especially want to start praying more when I am

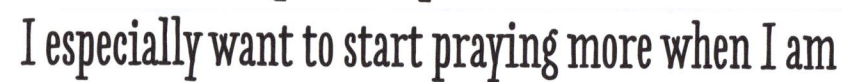

................................................................................. .

Amen.

## ISAIAH 40:31 TELLS US TO TRUST GOD'S PERFECT TIMING.

**Read the verse, and then doodle pictures to help you remember it.**

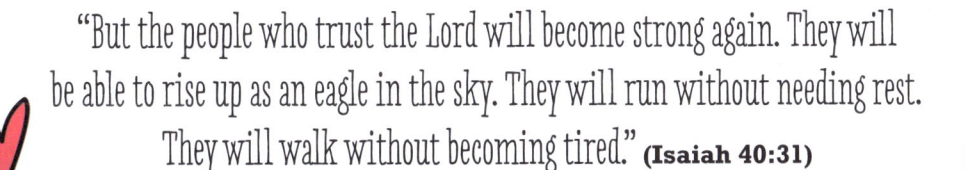

"But the people who trust the Lord will become strong again. They will be able to rise up as an eagle in the sky. They will run without needing rest. They will walk without becoming tired." **(Isaiah 40:31)**

GOD LOVES TO HEAR YOU LAUGH! HE LOVES US SO MUCH THAT HE INVENTED SMILING AND LAUGHING AND MAKES SURE THERE ARE FUNNY THINGS IN THE WORLD!

**Look up Proverbs 17:22 in your Bible and fill in the missing words.**

"A happy heart is like good .................... . But a .................... spirit drains your strength." **(Proverbs 17:22)**

48

# DID YOU KNOW THAT ALL CHRISTIANS BELONG TO GOD'S FAMILY? EVERY SINGLE PERSON WHO LOVES GOD IS ALSO YOUR BROTHER OR YOUR SISTER!

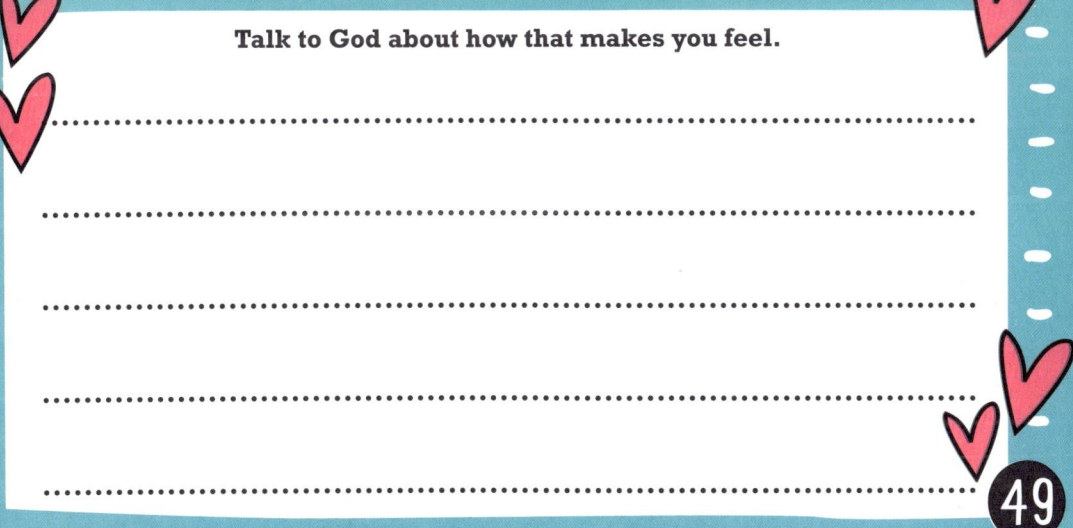

**Talk to God about how that makes you feel.**

## LOOK UP MATTHEW 6:28–29 IN YOUR BIBLE AND FILL IN THE MISSING WORDS.

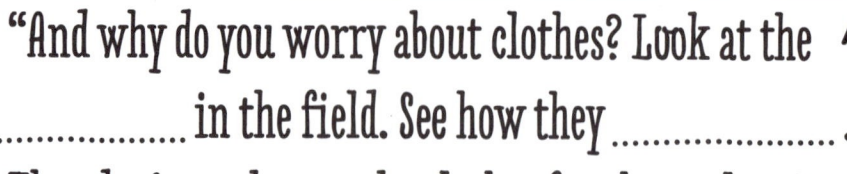

"And why do you worry about clothes? Look at the ........................ in the field. See how they ........................ . They don't work or make clothes for themselves."

**(Matthew 6:28)**

Who do you think provides for the plants and flowers in the wild?

..............................................

If God cares so much for the plants and flowers He created, just think how much He must care about you, His child!

50

## DID YOU KNOW THAT GOD THINKS YOU ARE COMPLETELY BEAUTIFUL?

When He made you, He didn't make any mistakes – He made you perfectly, according to His plan. Draw a picture of yourself, how God sees you!

# IN THE BIBLE, IT IS CLEAR THAT JESUS IS THE BEST LEADER BECAUSE HE IS ALWAYS GOOD, BRAVE, HONEST, CLOSE TO GOD, AND LEADS BY EXAMPLE.

**In your life, can you think of how setting an example may help you to lead others around you?**

SOMETIMES IT CAN BE HARD TO SAY SORRY, BUT TRY TO REMEMBER THAT GOD HAS FORGIVEN YOU FOR EVERY BAD THING YOU HAVE DONE (AND WILL CONTINUE TO DO SO), SO WE SHOULD TRY TO FORGIVE OTHERS IN THE SAME WAY!

**Look up Ephesians 4:32 and copy it down here.**

# GOD HAS CREATED MANY THINGS TO HELP KEEP US SAFE. WHEN YOU FEEL SCARED, REMEMBER GOD DOESN'T WANT YOU TO WORRY.

Look up Psalm 4:8 in your Bible, copy the verse here, and thank God for all the things in your life that keep you safe.

A GREAT WAY WE CAN HELP PEOPLE WHO ARE STRUGGLING IS BY TELLING GOD ABOUT THEM. PRAY THIS PRAYER FOR ANYONE YOU KNOW WHO NEEDS HIS HELP.

Dear God, thank You for always looking out for me and ...................... . Please help them through this difficult time. I pray that they feel Your love and comfort around them and do not feel alone. Please show me any way that I can help ...................... . Thank You. Amen.

# WRITE DOWN YOUR TOP FIVE WORDS THAT DESCRIBE GOD. EVERY TIME YOU FEEL SCARED OR WORRIED, READ THESE WORDS AND REMEMBER HOW INCREDIBLE GOD IS AND HOW MUCH HE LOVES YOU.

1. ..................................................................
2. ..................................................................
3. ..................................................................
4. ..................................................................
5. ..................................................................

# JESUS DIDN'T COME TO EARTH FOR HIS OWN SELFISH REASONS; HE CAME BECAUSE HE LOVES US AND WANTS TO SAVE US.

Think about the thing you least like doing. Who are you doing it for? Does it help someone else? Would it make God pleased if you did it with joy? Write down your thoughts here and ask God to help you.

## DO YOU COMPARE YOURSELF TO OTHERS? IT IS EASY TO LOOK AT WHAT OTHER PEOPLE HAVE AND THINK WE ARE NOT AS GOOD OR ARE BETTER THAN THEM.

In your Bible, look up Galatians 6:4–5, and make it personal by rewriting it here in the first person, using "I should," "I can," and "myself."

..................................................................................................

..................................................................................................

..................................................................................................

..................................................................................................

Don't forget, God has created you to be uniquely different. He has a very special path for you to follow!

# JESUS KNOWS THAT SOMETIMES WE FIND IT HARD TO KNOW THE RIGHT WORDS TO PRAY.

That is why He gave us the Lord's Prayer, which is written in Matthew 6:9–13 to help us pray. Read the Lord's Prayer aloud, and write down any bits you don't understand here.

..........................................................................................

..........................................................................................

..........................................................................................

..........................................................................................

Ask God, a parent, a teacher, or a youth worker to help you understand anything that confuses you.

# EVEN JESUS NEEDED TIME ALONE TO TALK TO GOD. AFTER HE HAD SPENT THIS TIME WITH HIS FATHER, HE ALWAYS KNEW EXACTLY WHAT HE SHOULD DO NEXT.

Read Mark 1:35–38, and write down where Jesus went to pray. Why do you think He chose to be alone?

..........................................................................................................

..........................................................................................................

..........................................................................................................

..........................................................................................................

# 1 CORINTHIANS 10:31 TELLS US THAT WE SHOULD DO EVERYTHING TO GLORIFY GOD.

**Think of the activity that you most like to do, and then write down how you can best give thanks and show God's love through it.**

# GOD'S LOVE FOR THE WHOLE WORLD IS AMAZING!

As a Christian, it is important to share the good news that God loves everyone so that others can feel His love too. Can you think of three people you could tell about God?

1 ....................................................................................

2 ....................................................................................

3 ....................................................................................

As you write down their names, think about the best way to do this and ask for God's help.

# WITHOUT CHEATING, TRY TO REMEMBER AS MANY OF THE TEN COMMANDMENTS AS YOU CAN AND WRITE THEM HERE!

1 .................................

2 .................................

3 .................................

4 .................................

5 .................................

6 .................................

7 .................................

8 .................................

9 .................................

10 ...............................

# DO NOT WORRY. GOD IS WITH YOU IN EVERYTHING YOU DO!

**Read Philippians 4:13 in your Bible, and draw a picture to help you remember what God is trying to say to you.**

# WHENEVER YOU FEEL LOST, DO NOT WORRY OR GET UPSET. REMEMBER THAT GOD IS WITH YOU ALWAYS.

**Read Joshua 1:9 in your Bible, and draw a picture to help you remember it.**

65

IT CAN BE VERY DIFFICULT TO BE KIND AND GOOD TO PEOPLE WE DO NOT GET ALONG WITH, BUT JESUS TELLS US IN MARK 12:31 THAT WE SHOULD LOVE PEOPLE AS WE LOVE OURSELVES, SO WE SHOULD DO OUR BEST TO TRY.

**Fill in this prayer.**

Dear God, thank You for loving me and always being by my side. I am finding it difficult to get along with ………………… at the moment. Please give me patience and courage and help me to behave in the best way I can. Amen.

# REMEMBER THAT GOD IS WITH YOU IN ALL THAT YOU DO. HE IS VERY PLEASED WITH YOU EVERY TIME YOU DO YOUR BEST.

**Fill in this prayer.**

Dear God, thank You for being there for me and wanting me to do the very best I can in my ................ competition. Please give me ................ , and help me to do my best to remember that everything I do, I do for You. Amen.

**CAN YOU THINK OF FIVE WORDS THAT WILL HELP YOU REMEMBER TO TRUST GOD?**

T .................
R .................
U .................
S .................
T .................

Even when you feel that God is not answering your prayers, you should always remember that He is the God of love. He will always give you what is best for you, when it is best for you. You can, and should, always trust Him.

68

# GOD CREATED US ALL FOR A SPECIAL PURPOSE! BECAUSE HE MADE YOU AND KNOWS YOU, HE HAS GREAT PLANS IN STORE FOR YOU. DOODLE WHAT YOU THINK GOD WANTS YOU TO DO WITH YOUR LIFE.

**Don't worry if you are not too sure of God's purpose for you yet. The best thing of all is that He will be guiding you every step of the way!**

69

# READ GENESIS 1:26–27. DID YOU KNOW THAT GOD MADE YOU IN HIS IMAGE?

This does not mean that you are God, but that you were created to be like Him and reflect what He is like. How would you like to be more like God? Think of three ways, and write them here, asking for His help.

1. ......................................................................................

2. ......................................................................................

3. ......................................................................................

70

**READ PSALM 139:13–16 IN YOUR BIBLE, THEN COPY THE WORDS THAT ARE MOST IMPORTANT TO YOU TO HELP YOU REMEMBER THEM.**

# GOD LOVES YOU, HEARS ALL YOUR PRAYERS, AND IS WITH YOU EVERY DAY, IN EVERYTHING YOU DO!

**Write your own prayer here and tell Him how thankful you are!**

Dear God...

...Amen.